Northern Nib

The Cully Baloney Counterfeiters

and other Barmy Ballads from Ireland!

Poetry by Robert E. Wilson
Illustrations by Aisling Wilson

Contents

Introduction

Thank you for picking up this bizarre book of barmy ballads! If your taste in poetry gravitates toward musing, meditative, metaphysical verse, then you've definitely chosen the ideal book... to steady that wobbly leg on your coffee table! However, if you simply want to read a few ballads written in lighter vein, you might enjoy what follows!

Historically, a ballad is a story told in verse. In this collection, I've taken a variety of themes and transformed them into ballads, each with a bit of humour. Some are based on the humorous situations we find in everyday life, whilst others are inspired by the anecdotes that in Ireland we call 'old yarns'. I'm also eager to show how a very simple idea can be developed into a complete piece of writing (in this case a poem, but it works for prose as well). Along with other material I've written, I'd be pleased if some of the ballads in this collection could be used as performance poetry or to encourage others to consider writing.

I'd like to thank a few people whose influence and support I've found extremely valuable: author and poet Lynda Tavakoli, the resourceful tutor of our writers' group, without whose encouragement (and homeworks) I'd never have reached this point; my fellow writers, for everything I've learned from them; literary agent Bill Jeffrey, whose wise counsel I always appreciate and last, but certainly not least, my daughter Aisling for the fascinating illustrations.

If you enjoy this collection, please tell your friends and look out for my other work; if not, then why not pass it on to someone who regularly gives *you* bizarre gifts – or is there still that wobbly coffee table?

Robert E. Wilson, June 2016.

About the author and artist:

Robert E. Wilson *is from County Antrim, Northern Ireland. An active member of an established writers' group, he contributed to the 'Linen Poetry & Prose Anthology' published in partnership with the Irish Linen Centre, Lisburn, which is available on Kindle. He is a regular reader at the 'Purely Poetry' evenings in the Crescent Arts Centre, Belfast, has participated in the Bard of Armagh Festival of Humorous Verse and was a finalist in the Connemara Mussel Festival Poetry Competition 2016, judged by the esteemed Irish poet Eamon Grennan.*
For further information on Robert's work, visit his website: www.northernnib.weebly.com or follow on Twitter @WilsonNib

Aisling Wilson *is an artist currently based in Northern Ireland, having graduated with a First Class Honours Degree in Fine Art from Ulster University and a Diploma in International Study from Waynesburg University, Pennsylvania, USA.*
For further information on Aisling's work, visit her website: www.aislingwilson.co.uk or follow on Twitter @awilsonartist

The Cullybackey Counterfeiters

a cautionary tale...

My first offering is built on a short anecdote I heard many years ago, with lots of my own details added. It's just one example of how a simple idea can be developed into a complete tale involving a couple of crazy characters, a dollop of daft dialogue and an altogether absurd ending!

Two lads from Cullybackey, Jim Hughes and Billy Crowe
Were always cooking up new ways to make a bit of dough;
I don't mean dough you *bake* with, no – *money* was their goal,
But don't be thinking they were flush – both lads were on the dole.

Now, though they were congenial to everyone they saw,
These boys would sometimes operate a bit outside the law,
Like when they drove a 'whippy' van, selling kids ice cream
Whilst, 'neath the counter, for the dads, were bottles of potcheen!

It's true most schemes the boys thought up were just 'pie in the sky'
But *sometimes*, they would hatch a plan that helped them to get by,
So it was not surprising when, one morning, Billy said,
'Hey, Jim, this wee idea's found its way into my head!

We want to make some money, right? Here's what we've got to do –
We'll forge a wheen o' bank notes and then, Jim, me and you
Can pass them off as genuine because they'll look so real;
Sure, it'll be dead easy, boy – there's no way we can fail!'

'Ach, man, we've got no printing press,' moaned Jim in Billy's ear.
'Well, I've it sorted,' Billy said. 'Remember Dave McTeer?
Our 'oul mate and his da had one – they used to print fake notes;
I mind they kept it in a shed, behind their pen of goats.'

Jim said, 'I can't believe you'd go to that clown and his da,
Yon couple o' buck eejits who live up near Buckna;
We can't afford to get this wrong, so let's just stay well clear
Of boys who'll make a hames o' things – the like o' Dave McTeer!'

'It's either him or nobody,' said Billy. 'Seriously,
They'll only have to *print* the notes to give to you and me,
Then we'll be really landed, Jim and, hey – just call me wacky –
But we'll end up the richest boys in all o' Cullybackey!'

'I guess it just *might* work,' said Jim, soon after he had thought
How they could slip some forged notes into everything they bought.
'Just think of all the *change* we'll get,' said Billy, 'for each fake –
Two fivers for a ten pound dud? Ach, it's a piece o' cake!'

So off they went then, to Buckna to visit Dave McTeer,
Armed with a stack of paper sheets that cost them pretty dear.
'Ach, how ya dooin', Davy? We've just come up from the town
To ask a favour,' Billy said. 'D'ye mind if we sit down?

Remember, Dave, thon printin' press you kept in your back shed?
Well, Jim and I have got this wee idea in our head;
We're wondrin' if you'd print for us a wheen o' notes in fake
And we'll give you a pound for say, each... *fifteen* that we make!'

'Okay, I'm game,' said Dave, 'I'll get things started right away,'
And told them that he'd bring it round by lunch that Saturday.
'I'll print you off about ten grand,' he added, as they went,
'But don't forget – I'll want *my* pound for every *fifteen* spent!'

Smiled Billy, as they headed back, 'Well, that's us on our way
To make a right wee fortune, Jim. Who said, *Crime doesn't pay?*
Ten thousand pounds in counterfeit – we're landed, boy, you know!'
And no-one was more happy than Jim Hughes and Billy Crowe.

On Saturday, just after twelve, a knock came at Jim's door,
And there was Dave, arms round a box, which he set on the floor.
'Well, there's your money, lads,' he said, 'and it won't be too hard
For you to calculate my cut, as promised in our yard.'

As soon as Dave went out the door, the two lads danced with glee!
'Let's have a look,' said Billy, with the box upon his knee.
They opened it, excited, then they both choked in their throats –
Ten thousand pounds were there okay – in crisp *fifteen-pound notes!*

Jim sifted through the box and groaned; to his dismay, he found
That, where each note looked real, its value stated, *Fifteen Pounds!*
'Aw, man, there's no such note as this! We're rumbled right away,
And three years in Maghaberry is where we'll get a stay!

Please tell me this is just a joke!' he whined, in dire despair,
As Billy stuck his head inside a cushion on the chair;
Snapped Jim, 'You wouldn't listen and you moaned I made a fuss
When I said we'd be nuts to let yon big galoot near us!

Well, I just hope you're satisfied! Just look at what he's done –
A box of perfect, crisp, forged notes but, no – we can't use one!
We'll not afford to buy more sheets to print a second lot,
So now our plans to get rich quick have all just gone to pot!'

They racked their brains for what to do, just how to sort this out,
But drew a blank at every turn, then Jim began to shout,
'I'm phonin' up yon Dave McTeer, who's caused us such distress,
To get up off his backside now and help us sort this mess!'

So, Jim picked up the telephone and spoke to Dave McTeer
In language highly colourful that can't be quoted here;
His anger turned to deep despair, then Dave said, 'Don't feel blue –
Here's one foolproof solution, boys, that I'll suggest to you:

There's a wee place down in Kerry where me da and me would go
To rid ourselves o' counterfeit, the pace there is so slow!
Their bank will always change for us whatever notes we bring;
Wee Paddy Doyle the banker? Ach, he'll never ask a thing!'

So, with very little money (well, at least, the legal kind),
The lads set off for Kerry, that wee special bank to find
But, with sufficient bus fare just to take them to Athlone,
The boys knew that they'd have to do the next part on their own.

Well, they cadged a lift to Cashel and another to Fermoy,
And chugged for ten miles in a tractor with a farmer's boy;
They lost directions once or twice and ended in Tralee,
But then they reached their destination – well, eventually!

They hobbled down the main street next to find a place to stay
And noticed that the local bank was not too far away.
'Let's head there in the morning,' Billy said, 'then we'll start back;
Now, I don't know about *you*, son – I want to hit the sack!'

Well, Jim and Billy slept like logs and morning came too soon,
In fact, the two lads didn't rise 'till almost afternoon;
They took the money in their case and headed down the street,
Then into that wee bank they walked and tried to look discreet.

'We've got ten thousand pounds with us, in fifteens, tied in wads
And are wonderin' if you'll exchange this money for us lads;
It would be right and handy, sir, if you could change them, please
For a wheen o' *smaller* bank notes we can use with greater ease.'

Without a word, wee Mr Doyle took all the notes they had
And placed them in his banker's safe, then this word he did add:
'If you come back here in an hour, I'll have it counted out.'
So, they headed to the pub next door to have a pint of stout.

When Jim and Billy came back in, their case was packed once more
And so they thanked wee Mr Doyle and headed out the door.
Asked Billy, 'Don't we need to check in case he's got it wrong?'
'Ach, no,' smiled Jim, 'Dave said he's honest as the day is long.'

They'd felt the journey down was bad, the one up home was worse;
They managed to hitch-hike a bit but this turned out a curse,
Like when they thought a driver said, 'I'm heading to *Armagh,*'
Then ended up in County Mayo – he'd said, *'Ballina!'*

Well, in the end, they made it back – but was that journey tough!
They'd detoured through most Irish counties, often sleeping rough;
At last a lorry driver took them, clinging to their loot,
To Cloughmills, where they had to walk the last ten miles on foot!

So, home at last, in Billy's house they found themselves once more,
Where both collapsed – one on a chair, the other on the floor;
Then, once recovered, they clicked open cans of ice-cold beers
To toast such new-found fortune and their plans to get rich: *'Cheers!'*

'And now, young Billy,' Jim announced, 'we've finally got our stash,'
As he unlocked the case to have a look at all their cash;
But, hey, what they discovered rendered speechless our two mates:
Half the case in *sevens* and the other half in *eights!*

Barking Mad!

a dog's 'tail'?

In Ireland, you must register for a licence in order to own a dog and it's against the law not to do so. Here's the tale of one persistent offender.

The tale that I shall now relay's
A simple one, in essence;
It's said that each dog has its day,
But not all have a licence!

My tale begins with local copper
Murphy – *Frank*, to some;
Our neighbourhood's crime stopper –
That's where I'm starting from.

Now, some days Frank's work is routine,
Complaints he often logs;
You know the sort of thing I mean:
Graffiti, noise – and *dogs!*

Well, residents in Chestnut Groves
Had gone a little crazy
And were complaining in their droves
About a dog called Daisy.

'Barking, thieving, chasing cars' –
Complaints ran on for pages;
'Pursuing cats through beds of flowers' –
She'd been a pest for ages.

The dog belonged to John McGurk
Who, though approaching fifty,
Had never done a full day's work –
Bone idle, if not shifty.

Well, PC Murphy knew wee John,
Frank's beat went down his road;
One day John's there, the next he's gone,
No proper fixed abode.

So Murphy went to find the lad
And have a conversation
(Not for the first time, I should add)
About the situation.

Eventually the constable
Saw wee John and his dog
And said, 'You must be sensible –
All these complaints I log..

..Will lead to many good folk here,
Especially those with gardens,
Taking action, John, I fear,
And phoning up the wardens!

So, John, you must control your dog
And, let me tell you straight,
If she ends up inside the pound,
The owner's charge is great.

And, finally, I want to say
That you will need to go
And buy a licence straight away –
Ten times I've told you so.'

'Now, back off, cop,' came John's reply,
'You know my situation –
We're stony broke, and that's no lie,
Both me and my Alsatian.'

Then Murphy said, 'Stop answering
Me back, and don't be funny;
If necessary, sell a thing
To help you raise the money..

..And bring to me that licence soon –
No further hesitation;
I want it on my desk at noon
Next Thursday, at the station.'

Well, PC Murphy didn't think
That wee McGurk would listen;
'Twas much more likely, with a wink
He'd say, 'Me dog's gone missin'!'

So, picture Murphy's great surprise
As noon on Thursday beckoned;
McGurk appeared before his eyes –
'Twas not what he had reckoned!

Without a word, wee John produced
A paper from his pocket,
Which PC Murphy soon deduced
Was not some random docket.

Frank said, 'Now give that form to me,
I didn't think you'd make it.'
Still, Murphy read it carefully
In case he'd tried to fake it.

But no, it seemed that all was fine –
On close examination,
The licence looked quite genuine
For Daisy the Alsatian.

Then wee McGurk said, 'You were right
And I'd no choice as well,
So I decided late last night
On something I could sell.'

'So, you were able,' Murphy sighed,
'To find a thing to flog?'
'Ach, that was simple,' John replied,
'I went and sold the dog!'

Neither Rhyme
Nor Reason

a tale of one poet's struggle with blank verse...

'There was an old man from Tralee,
Who was stung on the nose by a... hornet!'

When I sat down to write a poem,
Without fail, every time,
I'd always gone to dreadful lengths
To make the darn thing rhyme!

Suppose the first line ended, 'king',
The second ended, 'queen',
I'd end the third with 'ring' or 'sing'
Or 'thing'. See what I mean?

'Why does this have to be?' I asked,
'We don't converse like that!
Imagine how absurd we'd sound
Had we to rhyme our chat!'

If rhyming talk became the norm,
Oh, what a situation –
To speak in verse and have to rhyme
Our every conversation!

If 'next door' chirped, 'Cold weather –
See the ice on both our cars?'
I'd have to think of something quick:
'Yes, freezing – just like Mars!'

So I grew quite determined
When I lifted up my pen,
To dodge a rhyme at any cost –
(Sigh!) There I go again!

I said, 'I'll join a writing class
To help me in my plight,
Held in the local library
At eight, each Tuesday night.'

But first I set a daunting task
And looked for inspiration
That, for my first class, I'd create
A literary blank creation!

I said, 'I'll write about my trip
To Athens, late last Spring;
Those place-names and the ancient sites
Won't rhyme with anything!'

I persevered both night and day
And went to every length
To stretch my skills to maximum
And keep each stanza blank!

With attention paid to rhythm
And vocabulary and tone,
I started to appreciate
That blank verse stands alone..

..And realised, to my surprise,
It didn't sound so bad;
In fact, if I heard one more rhyme
I'd go forever...*crazy!*

So, to the class I promptly went
And sat down on the right.
The tutor asked, 'Have you a piece
You'd like to read tonight?'

I proudly said, 'My poem describes
The Greek Acropolis!'
She smiled and said, 'My name is Greek –
It's Papadopoulis!'

Secret of a Happy Marriage

a suspicious tale...

A tale about an apparently conventional, mainstream couple without mystery or secret. That is, until you explore their attic!

The Rileys, Mike and Jane

Were considered, in the main,

A middle-class, suburban, ordered couple;

Lives compartmentalized,

No thing sensationalised,

Their taste not garish, rather safe and subtle.

It seemed like wedded bliss:

Her birthday he'd not miss,

They both had time for work, for play, for rest;

Their relationship transparent,

No secrets were apparent,

Except, that was, for one old wooden chest.

In a corner of the attic

An item sat there static,

A chest of wood that Mike had not explained;

He called it his old crock

But he never would unlock

This chest, or say what it contained.

It mystified poor Jane

Who sometimes would complain

To friends about her husband's strange old crock –

'The first week we were married,

That crock upstairs he carried

And, to this day, he's kept it under lock.'

In certain times of tension,

If the crock Jane dared to mention,

Mike dismissed it in a manner quite off-hand;

He'd not give in to coercion

But create a clear diversion

In the conversation, back to something bland.

With his trendy Gucci suit

Packed carefully in the boot,

Mike was off one day to business in Tralee;

Just before he turned to go,

He told Jane he'd miss her so,

But he'd be back on Thursday, before tea.

With Mike away on business
(He was a rep. For Guinness),
Jane thought she'd have his other suit dry-cleaned;
He'd be doubtless pleased to learn
It was fresh on his return,
So to get it from his wardrobe rail she leaned.

As the suit she lifted down,
Jane had a good feel round
To make sure that no money, card or docket
Would be in it at 'Smart Suits'
(That's the cleaners opposite Boots),
And felt an object in his inside pocket.

Well, Jane foraged all around
So this item could be found,
With passing interest in what it might be;
Then, on an ornate ring,
Tied to one short piece of string,
Was a dark, metallic, antiquated key.

Though it beat all definition,
Jane's female intuition
Caused her to think of what this might unlock;
With Mike gone until tomorrow,
The key she thought she'd borrow
And try to find out if it cracked the crock!

Well, filled with curiosity,
She pocketed the key
And braced herself for what she soon might find
And, while just a little scared,
To be thoroughly prepared,
She grabbed a glass and poured herself some wine.

Then, in great anticipation
Mixed with certain trepidation,
The key in one hand, Merlot in the other,
To the attic Jane did go
And, with one click, what did you know?
The lock was open, without any bother!

With cold shivers down her spine
And another gulp of wine,
Jane placed her fingers underneath the lid;
Though alone, she glanced around
Then, whilst kneeling on the ground
She pushed it up, to see just what it hid.

Well, Jane gasped in great surprise
And could not believe her eyes
As the contents of the crock came into view;
She could never have foretold
That, in this wooden chest so old
Lay two spanners, very shiny and brand new!

Now Jane couldn't understand
Just exactly what Mike planned
With these spanners, as no actual sense it made:
'It's not like he was handy,
Just like his cousin Andy,
Selling tools within the joinery trade.'

Then something caught Jane's eye –

In the crock, what did she spy?

A folded sack in which was neatly hid

A truly massive stash –

Why, ten thousand pounds in cash,

In wads of fivers, each worth sixty quid!

At this, Jane *was* concerned –

Had this money all been earned

Through some clandestine, shady business deal?

The chest she locked again,

But the mystery did remain

And, if she confronted Mike, how would he feel?

When Mike's suit came back next day,

Jane returned it straight away –

The *key*, that is, to where it had been found;

This way, he mightn't guess,

Or should she just confess

To having borrowed it to snoop around?

As Mike's return drew nigh,

Jane heaved a mighty sigh

And tried to cast the findings from her mind,

But once his car pulled up outside

She knew *that* time had now arrived,

Though she'd wait until they both were wined and dined.

So, with a fond embrace

Jane showed him to his place

In the dining room, where she'd prepared good fare

But, as coffee she did pour,

She could hold things back no more

And said to Mike, 'You know that suit you wear…'

Well, with one enormous gulp,

And feeling she had turned to pulp,

Jane said to Mike that, accidentally,

Whilst looking for a docket

She'd found, in his suit pocket

This curious and interesting key.

Now, although Jane did insist
That she'd tried hard to resist
What surely was an obvious temptation,
She was sorry now to tell
That, just like Eve, this lady fell,
And given in to her imagination!

Well, Mike listened to it all
Then, whilst staring at the wall
Said, pensively, 'Well, now that *you've* confessed,
I suppose that I was wrong
To hide the truth from you so long,
So please listen – let me put your mind at rest:

Dear, each time you made me sad,
Or downright flaming mad
And I wanted to divorce you, there and then,
Instead, here's what I'd do –
I'd take a trip to B&Q,
Buy a spanner and then come back home again!'

'Mike,' Jane said, 'what noble manners
That you only bought *two* spanners
In all our twenty years of married life;
But… that *ten grand* in the sack,
Rolled up there, at the back,
If not explained, might cause us needless strife.'

'Well,' sighed Mike, 'it's not *quite* true
That I only purchased *two*,
But to hide those spanners seemed to me a crime;
Every time I had a dozen,
I passed them to my cousin,
Who sold them off – a fiver at a time!'

Mixed Messages

Based on a joke by Rev Joe Mooney
in his book 'Joe's Jokes'.

an ecclesiastical tale...

The connection between the preacher in this tale and any cleric I've ever known is purely coincidental! (A Session Clerk is the name given to the senior elder in some non-conformist churches).

Reverend Phil McGarry, from a wee town near the Bann,
Spent five years up in Belfast to become a clergyman
So, youthful and exuberant, with many skills to hone,
He waited for a calling to a church all of his own.

Well, Phil was asked to preach one Sunday morning, late in May
At Connors Hill, a country church, a fair wee bit away
And, with excitement bordering at times on trepidation,
In order to impress them, he made careful preparation.

Now, once Phil mentioned *Connors Hill*, the Rev Cecil Miles,
His overseer and mentor, gave him one of his wry smiles.
'Phil,' he said, 'I'll warn you that some preachers they might "roast"
But, if the folk there like you, you're a better man than most!

Now, please don't get me wrong, young Phil, the congregation there
Are good, devout, industrious folk and always very fair,
So If you're preaching's sound, they'll say, but if you keep them late,
Or don't stick firmly to their rules, they'll tell you – good and straight!'

Well, the day for Connors Hill arrived and Phil felt well prepared,
Though, underneath, he was a little – *just* a little – scared;
His fears, however, were allayed as he approached the place
And there stood Jim, the Session Clerk, a smile upon his face.

He did still slightly wonder, though, just what might lie in store,
From what he'd heard those preachers say who'd been along before.
'My name's Jim Boyd,' the old man said. 'You're very welcome here
But, if you don't mind, let me have a quick word in your ear:

The good folk here at Connors Hill are punctual, you should know,
All seated by eleven, but by twelve they'll want to go;
With meals to cook and farms to work, it's hardly that surprising,
So don't be keeping them all day with too much sermonising!'

Well, Phil began the service with a good old rousing hymn,
Then thanked them for their welcome, with a special word for Jim;
He stuck to what he had prepared, just what he'd planned to do,
And started preaching at 11.30, right on cue.

Then, twenty minutes later, he was ready to conclude,
But there was just *one* other point he thought was rather good,
So he tagged it on his message, an effective punch to pack
And heard a 'Hallelujah!' from a pew some ten rows back.

Now, preachers like to know they're striking chords with all who hear,
So to get that 'Hallelujah' filled his spirit with good cheer;
He thought, 'The folk must like my message; maybe just before
The final hymn and benediction, I'll add something more!'

So, Phil drew breath and carried on, his message to expand;
Indeed, he preached much longer than originally planned
And, as more 'Hallelujahs' echoed round the congregation,
It staggered Phil to think his preaching caused such jubilation!

When Phil next glanced up at the clock, *a solid hour* he'd preached,
So he exclaimed 'Amen!' as his conclusion he'd now reached
And, exhausted yet encouraged, one last hymn he then announced,
And, with a happy smile, the benediction he pronounced.

It seemed the folk were eager to get home from church that day,
(Indeed, I wouldn't like to have been standing in their way),
While Phil, filled with elation, grinned as wide as he was able,
As one who'd surely sparked discussion round each dinner table!

Well, Jim, the Clerk then came across, once all the folk had left
And, of that smile he'd earlier worn, his face was now bereft,
But yet the old man's changed demeanour Phil did not detect
And said, 'I can't believe how much into that talk I packed!'

'You preached a long time,' Jim replied. 'I told you at the start,
Come twelve o'clock, the good folk here are ready to depart;
You kept them there 'till almost one, so you can now be sure
That, probably they'll never have you back through this church door.'

'That's not the signal I was getting,' Phil said, in surprise.
'The congregation liked me, it was plain before my eyes;
In fact, it seemed the more I said, the more they wished to hear,
With all those shouts of "Hallelujah" ringing in my ear!

Indeed, I planned to stop on time, but each new point I made
And, "Hallelujah!" someone in the congregation said,
And so, with such encouragement, I'd find *more* words to say,
To leave folk feeling really blessed as they went home today!'

'Young man,' said Jim, 'At Connors Hill, they never sulk or strunt,
They're straight and honest, as I've said and always very blunt;
Did you think that the good folk here were shouting, "Hallelujah"?
You should have listened better – they were saying, *"That'll do ya!"'*

My Turn

a tipsy tale...

It's a 'hen party' and, as not everyone has met before, each person has been asked to say a few things about herself, not forgetting her school, career, loves and a few secrets.

All right, okay, it's round to me:
My name is Mary Ann Magee,
And what you get is what you see –
I think!

I've had a little much to drink,
Though not enough to make me sink,
But from this challenge I'll not shrink –
Here goes!

You've asked us all, dear Alice Rose
To share some things that no-one knows.
Is this to keep us on our toes?
You cow!

So what things can I tell you now,
That wouldn't land me in a row
Because I've kept them close till now?
Let's see…

I'm forty; okay, *forty-three*,
I'm working for a company
Called Green's, you know it, old C. T.
It's – *great!*

My school? Eastfield Collegiate,
A bubbly girl but always late;
Met my first boyfriend at the gate –
I know.

I always had a steady flow
Of suitors. Where did they all go?
I guess I was a bit too slow
To act.

A handsome man I'd never lack,
But I thought love would hold me back
From my career. Was I correct?
Don't say.

But look at where I am today,
The Head of Finance – that's okay;
I wouldn't like to state my pay –
Not bad.

'Always work hard,' said my dad.
When I was young, it drove me mad!
But now you'll say, 'She's old and sad,'
Alone.

But, hey! I don't think I should moan,
I love the freedom on my own,
I call the shots and set the tone,
Juste moi.

Have I a certain 'je ne sais quoi?'
You know I've studied opera,
And ridden in a gymkhana.
It's true.

Where do I live? - In Castle View,
My house is number twenty-two;
I stretched my cash for somewhere new
And nice.

I've found success and paid the price,
Though I could have been married *twice*;
Well, now to add a little spice –
Don't swoon…

Our firm's Director leaves this June,
The post is up for grabs quite soon,
They've tipped me and I'm o'er the moon!
Nice stuff.

Interviews? Why, I can bluff
And, when I have to, I'll talk tough!
Well, maybe I have said enough.
But, hey!

I swear, I'd give it all away –
The job, the home, the horse, the pay,
If I could just move in today –
Next door.

You'll say, 'This actress likes the floor,
I wish she'd just get to the core;
What new surprise has she in store
Tonight?'

I've said too much already, right?
I should've kept my lips more tight,
Performing under my spotlight,
On cue.

Girls, I'm in love, uh-huh, it's true –
He's living up in Castle View,
Next door to my place, 'twenty-two',
With *her.*

Well, girls, his woman sure is rare,
She should be on 'What Not To Wear';
Together they're the oddest pair
I've seen.

I guess you'll think I'm kind of mean,
She's forty, but thinks she's a teen,
I just wish she was off the scene --
Goodbye!

Good riddance, too, I say, and why?
That stuck-up floozie makes me cry
Because she's with the only guy
I want!

Well, call me jealous, let me rant,
Some girls will score, while others shan't,
But where did he find *her*? I can't
Decide.

He's charming, that can't be denied,
But *she*? I know this might sound snide,
Was born the day that good taste died.
Nast-ee!

Now him and her just don't agree,
I think she's jealous as can be,
She hates it when he speaks to *me*.
My word!

He says her sister, called Meg Ford,
Might be appointed to Green's board,
If that's the case, I'm good as floored –
Dead meat.

Imagine me, there, in that seat,
At interview, pristine and neat;
Would floozie's sister be discreet?
Yeah, right!

My future I've no doubt she'd blight,
'Magee, a woman of the night,
Whose motives aren't so snowy white,'
She'll spout.

I'll bet Meg Ford is brassy, stout,
Just like her sister. I've no doubt
That she'll believe the lies about
Old me.

So, that's my turn. As you can see,
I've been quite candid, bold and free!
Now, who's the person next to me?
Meg Ford?!

Keep your Eye on the Ball

...and not some 'wee doll'!

'Some people believe football is a matter of life and death; I am very disappointed with that attitude. I can assure you it is much, much more important than that.'

Bill Shankly

a sporting tale...

When my mate Tommy fell in love
It sure got up my nose;
He gave his mates a hefty shove
To make way for young Rose!

In fairness, that wee girl was nice,
Her looks and charm appealed,
But we all feared she would entice
Him off the football field.

You see, our Tom, he was the star
Of Railway Street FC,
A player who was just the best, bar
Stevie Strong – and me!

Well, our worst fears were realised
Before we'd time to blink,
When he failed to materialise
In Dobbins, for a drink.

We always met there after practice
On a Tuesday night;
The craic and blarney helped connect us –
Kept the balance right.

Then, once wee Rose came, Tom was never
In old Dobbins found,
Though, to be frank, he hardly ever
Bought us all a round!

But that's not all, it wasn't just
The Dobbins bit he missed –
His attendance at the practice must
Have been worst on the list!

It bothered us – it really did,
The way he let us down,
For Tommy clearly was the best mid-
Fielder in the town.

Then one night Tommy came along,
So full of love's young bliss,
And said to me and Stevie Strong,
'You'd best sit down for this...

I've asked wee Rose to marry me!
I want you to remember
And make sure that you both keep free
The nineteenth of September!'

Then Stevie said – and I agreed –
'Hey, Tom, you'd better watch,
For that sounds like a day when we'd
Be playing in a match!'

As if this wasn't bad enough,
He looked at me, dead pan,
And said, 'My old mate, Billy Duff –
I want you for best man!'

Well, much as I was flattered
To fulfil this special role,
I knew that I'd be shattered
In body, mind and soul...

I'd have to spend more time with Tom
Than Railway Street FC,
And whispered low to Stevie Strong,
'How nice,' sarcastically.

I wasn't miffed because I knew
Romance came to Tom's door,
But it was just that, in my view,
He should love *football* more!

Ach, I agreed; and then he said,
'So now the fine best man
Must meet my Rose's bridesmaid
And twin sister, Julie Ann.'

Now, frankly, things went better
Than I ever thought they would;
The day ran to the letter –
Well, as best a wedding could!

And soon our Tom was fighting fit,
And back in Dobbins too,
Though I skived off that year a bit,
With other things to do.

Well, now at Railway Street FC
Are two boys each fan knows,
Great super-strikers, I must say –
Those twins of Tom and Rose!

But, our *real* stars, and I'm not wrong,
A back and midfield man,
Are twins who proudly now belong
To me – and Julie Ann!

Penny For Your Thoughts

a financial tale...

*A*nother ballad based on a 'yarn' I once heard. This fellow makes Ebenezer Scrooge seem free with his cash!

It started with a piggy bank when he was just a boy,
He guarded it more jealously than any other toy;
With pennies he soon filled it
And, as though some power instilled it
In his mind, a little miser was young Roy.

Roy Farthing (what a truly fitting name for this young man),
Spent almost all his childhood hatching up a savings plan;
While his brothers all played football
And his sister had a ragdoll,
He'd sit and count his money with his gran.

Roy's granny gave him this advice while he was still at school:
'Save your money carefully – make thriftiness your rule.'
He took her word to heart, then,
And thought if he should part, then
With a single pound by chance, he'd be a fool.

Now thriftiness is one thing, but Roy took it much too far –
Once his piggy bank was full, he saved his money in a jar;
He counted it each week night
And it would be a bleak night
If he had to spend some cash – oh was he sour!

Well, this continued through his teens – the one thing in his head,
And jars gave way to boxes that he kept beneath his bed;
He made money his obsession
And his most esteemed possession
Was a book on commerce he forever read.

So, Roy went into banking, which was not at all surprising,
Given that his job was, for the most part, spent devising
Plans to help folk with their savings
And to hold back any cravings
To spend, or do extravagant up-sizing.

Now, well might we all wonder, with this focus on finance,
How Roy could ever find the time to cultivate romance,
But he met young Penny Weller,
Who got a job as teller
In the bank where he was working, just by chance.

So, Roy asked Penny out and then spent ages looking smart,
While having second thoughts, as with some cash he'd have to part;
Then he picked a posy, rose-red
From his next-door-neighbour's flowerbed
To help him – cheaply – win the lady's heart!

Now, it should have told young Penny something of this canny man
That the meal for two turned out to be the local chippy van
And, if that was not too much,
Roy then added, 'Let's go Dutch,'
Which from that day on, remained his payment plan.

In spite of all his meanness, Penny found our Roy quite charming
And headed down the aisle next year as Mrs Penny Farthing!
Though appropriately named,
She soon came to feel ashamed
That her husband's cheapskate ways were so alarming!

Sure, Roy was tighter than a drum, the banknote was his god
And, as for spending cash, he'd rather face a firing-squad!
Yes, the very rich Roy Farthing
Kept his family on a shoe-string,
Which inevitably left them overawed.

Roy's love affair with money blossomed while the market thrived
But, once the banking crisis loomed, his general mood just dived
And said, amidst his ravings,
Regarding his life's savings,
The dreaded day he'd planned for had arrived!

So, to his local bank he rushed, like one who'd lost the plot
And, in a single swoop, our anxious Roy withdrew the lot
Then, in cash, he placed it all
In a safe inside the wall,
Behind a picture of his Granny, Dot.

Now, not long after this took place, Roy's health was dealt a blow
But still, this didn't once distract him from his stack of dough,
For he said, 'Dear Penny, tell me,
That you'll take it all, entirely,
And bury it beside me when I go!'

Well, Roy expressed his dying wish that, sealed within his coffin,
Would be the vast sum that he'd saved, and mentioned this so often
That Penny, just to please him
And, from his suffering, ease him,
Agreed, yet still his mindset wouldn't soften.

Of course poor Penny, tired and weary of her frugal life,
Now really felt she'd paid the price of being a miser's wife
And next, to top the lot,
Deep in a graveyard plot
Would rest the fortune that would ease her strife.

Again her spirit was brought down, no feelings of elation
When, in his final hour, Roy passed to her the combination
That would unlock the cash
That he felt compelled to stash,
To Penny and her family's consternation.

But Penny stuck by what she'd promised – on the day Roy died
And without hesitation, she with Roy's request complied;
At the graveside she was calm,
Just as quiet as a lamb
And never once for man or money cried.

Well, this brings me to yesterday. She's just back from a cruise,
And said she'd dined just like a queen and drank expensive booze!
As she got into her Merc,
I asked, 'Penny, did you shirk
That promise to old Roy? What was your ruse?'

'I kept my promise,' Penny said, 'but good sense I don't lack –
Once I had got Roy's money, to the bank I headed back,
Where I opened an account,
And lodged the full amount,
And then, into his coffin, dropped a *cheque!*'

Going up? Going down? It's Donna Brown!

a tale of highs and lows...

The musings of a lift attendant (elevator operator) in a big department store.

Life, as we know, has many highs and lows,
A lot of ups and downs,
But mine has more than anyone here knows –
My name is Donna Brown.

I'm sure I've met a few of you before;
Let's see if you can guess
The place where you have stepped inside my door.
I tease, I must confess!

So, *here's* my puzzle – can you work it out?
I don't go *far* each day,
But yet I travel *miles*, I shouldn't doubt,
And stop but never stay!

You'll guess my job before I say much more!
Each morning, night and noon
You'll find me in a big department store –
And work out *where* quite soon!

I like it there; most folk use me a bit,
The trendy and the squares,
Unless, of course, they're feeling very fit
And choose to take the stairs!

I meet all types – the great, the good, the old,
The young, the big, the small;
Some chat, some joke, some tease, some moan, some scold!
Trust me, I've met them all.

Some people come to view our winter clearance,
Or just the store to see,
But I hope it's an UP-lifting experience
To be in here with me!

There are a lot who just say, 'Second Floor,'
Then I've some chatty friends
Who tell me all the gossip of the store
Before their journey ends!

I like to be well groomed. I must look chic
For staff and shoppers both,
And friends now joke that I have come to speak
Weeth mahbles een may mowth!

When my door opens, who'll be standing there?
I don't know who I'll see;
I like most folk, but one or two can scare,
If it's just them and me!

Yet I'll take them to the basement or the top,
No matter who I meet;
I'm conscious that I represent this shop
And *always* am discreet..

..When people tell me things I shouldn't hear,
Like nosey Mrs Dick;
Would I repeat the half of it? No fear!
But someone I can't stick..

..Is that 'madam' from the office, Mrs Truss
Who always thinks that she
Is just a cut or two above the rest of us,
And mostly little me.

She doubtless thinks that all I do in here
Is...well, just flick some switch;
I'm sure she says I'm just some dizzy blonde.
At least I'm no old witch!

Where *did* she cast her evil spell today?
I think she went to 'Lights';
'Good riddance – don't come back!' I'd like to say,
'I'm off to greater heights!'

Then last Christmas, who stepped in here but *John Fee,*
The top floor *Romeo!*
Well, before I said, 'Good morning, sir,' he *kissed* me,
Beneath some mistletoe!

Well, I felt rather special! What a guy!
I dreamed that I could travel
Up and up until I reached the sky!
But... my dream would soon unravel..

..As, 'John kissed *every* girl,' said Mary Hughes
From Carpets, with much mirth,
'In Furniture, Cosmetics, Bags and Shoes!'
(Well – *that* brought me down to earth!)

My scariest time here? – One day when we
Broke down. How did I stand
Being stuck somewhere between floors two and three
With Sales Clerk Katie Brand?

Well, you would have thought that she was on Titanic,
The way she screamed and roared;
I'm surprised she didn't start a full-scale panic –
I wished I could have floored..

..Her with my shoe, to keep the shoppers calm –
A tempting thing to do!
But I'd have ended up before old Sam,
Our mighty boss, McHugh.

So, I just did my best to reassure
My passengers that day
Above the din, that I was very sure
Some help was on the way.

I could have strangled her, but stayed professional;
I know this sounds bizarre –
We Methodists don't go to the confessional,
Or I'd have spent an hour!

But, thankfully, most days are less dramatic,
The atmosphere is grand;
But I admit, I still feel post-traumatic
When in steps Katie Brand!

At times like Christmas, though, it's push and shove
And when the sales are on,
All that I hear is, 'Room for one more, love?'
I'm glad when folk are gone!

Though, other times, I feel a bit alone
When my door closes shut;
I've no close colleagues. Ach – I shouldn't moan,
Or am I in a rut?

Well, actually, there is a girl called Ursa,
Next door, just to my right;
But when I'm up, she's down – and 'visa-versa',
Ships passing in the night!

I tell myself that leave this place I *must*
And join the world outside;
They say I'm needed here, but am I just
Being taken for a ride?

And then I think I'm safe within this place,
From hustle, noise and babble;
Each morning I don't come to work to face
Some departmental squabble!

But, when all's said and done, it's rather fun
To work in this great store;
That's why I have a smile for *everyone*
Who steps in through my door!

And I *love* it when you *mirror* my expression –
Smile back at Donna Brown,
As I ask *you* that all-important question:
'Going up or going down?'

Love or Money?

a romantic tale (?)

The story of a rather posh lady, as told by her long-suffering brother.

I've a slightly younger sister, name of Madeline de Vere,
Who's facing a momentous choice, which I shall soon make clear;
A very well-healed, stylish lady, worth a lot of bob,
But you can make your own mind up if Maddy is a *snob!*

She lives at number thirty, Ashbourne Manor, if you please,
A place where you'll need half a million just to own the keys;
She hasn't worked a day for years – to her, life's having fun,
Part financed by her former husbands: three and two and one!

For anyone who hasn't met her, Madeline is rare,
Once seen and not forgotten – a flamboyant gal, I swear!
Three times divorced, with fifty knocking loudly at the door,
And definitely on the scent of husband number four!

Oh, by the way, I'm Richard – Maddy's brother, as I've said,
Though certain that, from different moulds the two of us were made;
Well, anyhow, this brings me to the gossip of the day –
How Maddy's latest conquest is now clearly underway!

It seems to walk the aisle *again* our Maddy thinks is fine,
(Oh, by the way, don't call her that – she's always *Madeline!*)
The problem is, this time she doesn't know what she should do,
As there is not just *one* potential husband here, but *two*!

The first one is called Harry, and she has me understand
He's a property developer, who owns a lot of land;
She met him at a concert, through a friend in real estate
And, after cocktails in the bar, she asked him on a date.

The second is a chap called Dan, a cashier in the bank
(Which Madeline admits is just a bit beneath her rank);
But anyhow, his looks and charm have blown her quite away,
So much so that she does some banking almost every day!

So, there she is, our Maddy, with *two* suitors for her hand,
But far from revelling in the fact that she's in big demand,
Ms Madeline is ruminating morning, noon and night,
As to which her heart she'll give, and which she'll put to flight!

Now, if you've met my sister, then you'll know just what I mean,
Our Madeline is every bit the classic drama queen;
'Oh, dear,' she'll say, 'I'm really torn between these two fine chaps –
Who should it be – my *charming knight*, or *millionaire*, perhaps?

Dear Dan seems so romantic, he could sweep me off my feet,
Yet doesn't have much ready cash, which I won't find so sweet,
And though our Harry is a taste that I may not acquire,
He'll keep me in the lifestyle to which I so much aspire.'

Well, listening to Maddy with such regularity
Was nearly driving me insane – I think that's plain to see;
I'd tried advising her *this* way, and *that*, without success,
Then hit upon one last resort – quite daft, I must confess.

It started off like all my visits, cordial and polite,
Then Maddy steered the chat round to the topic of the night;
She sighed, 'Oh, Richard, my dilemma is becoming chronic,'
As she poured me a glass of wine, herself a gin and tonic.

Well, I know for a fact that Maddy always reads her stars,
Though she would never *say* that she believes in psychic powers!
So, having no ideas left, I ventured to suggest
A simple course of action that might put her mind at rest.

I'd heard some girls in work say that they'd seen a fortune-teller,
(Most probably to find out when they'd meet their perfect *feller!*)
It seems this lady's famous – why, her name was known to *me*,
So *Maddy* would have heard of her – enchanting *Mona Lee*.

'Now, Madeline,' I said, 'you have a mystic side, I know,
And I've heard *love* is in the air if you're a Scorpio;
So, why not trust the stellar powers and bring your quandary
To Mona Lee, who has "the gift", and hear what she might say?

I know some folk who've gone to her and they would swear to you
She accurately can foretell events that will come true,'
Well, Maddy sat and listened with a look of disbelief.
(I'm surprised she couldn't tell that I was lying through my teeth!)

Of course she put resistance up, threw back her head and laughed,
'I simply don't believe that stuff – the whole idea's daft:
"You'll see a handsome stranger with a dashing, curled moustache."
Oh, Richard, you know it's a load of crystal balderdash!

I don't know what's come over you,' she nonchalantly said,
'The thought of doing such a thing is *never* in my head;
In fact, that's quite the daftest thing you've *ever* said to me,'
Then rolled her eyes and poured herself another 'G&T'.

I think I know my sister well and so I let things rest,
(She's always sure to change her mind whenever she gets stressed)
And, right enough, in two days' time, she called me on the phone,
But speaking in a quieter, less condescending tone.

'Now, Richard, dear,' she said, 'about our chat the other night,
Concerning my two gentlemen, I *still* don't know who's right;
Well, please don't think I'm mad, but out of curiosity
And *nothing else*, I'll go along and see that Mona Lee.'

I smiled and thought, 'Relief!' the moment I switched off the phone!
'Perhaps now Madeline will leave the rest of us alone!
In spite of all the scepticism she voiced at the start,
If I know Maddy, she will take what Mona says to heart!'

Once Maddy's set her cap on *one* man, she will try her best
To do whatever she must do to make sure he's impressed,
(Though when she gets her hands on him, a *pitied* man he'll be!)
And then she phoned to tell me of her date with Mona Lee.

So, Maddy took a lift with me when her appointment came,
But warned, 'If I hear something nasty, Richard, you're to blame;
Although I you told you earlier it's all a lot of tosh,
I want a nice prediction, if I'm paying her some dosh.'

She said she'd meet me for a coffee afterwards, at two
But, when I got there, Maddy said, 'I've fallen out with you!'
Indeed, her mood appeared so cross, so far from bright and chatty,
I don't know which was steaming most, the lady or the latte!

Eventually, she rubbed her brow, then looked at me and said,
'The next time you've a bright idea, keep in in your head!'
'Are you upset,' I asked, 'at something Mona could foresee?'
'Well, no,' said Maddy, 'more at *what remark* she made to me.

I told the lady, "Frankly, I am sceptical of this,
But allowed myself to be persuaded," if she got the gist;
Then next I asked, "How should I pay a person, well – like you?
Am I to cross your palm with silver? Will a cash card do?"

And, yes, I said she ought to hear the reason I was there,
How I'm facing a dilemma that I simply cannot bear;
Who was to be the lucky man, which one was I to marry –
The handsome heartthrob that is Dan or largely-loaded Harry?

She closed her eyes, which I imagine helped her concentration,
Whilst I sat in, I must admit, some slight anticipation,
Then, finally, she said to me (which I did not find funny),
"There's a question you must answer: *Do I wed for love or money?*

I'm getting vibes so strong that I won't need a crystal ball;
Yes, I clearly can foretell a lavish wedding in the fall.
I see you walking down the aisle and there's a lucky man –
The one you'll wed is Harry, but the *lucky* one is Dan!'"

Perhaps Next Week
More thoughts from Mary Ann Magee.

a wistful tale...

I liked this character and thought I'd revive her for a second ballad.

Another Friday night and here I am, all on my own,
Sat in the Emerald Bar;
Well, my best friend, Alice Rose
Will be here. When? Heaven knows –
Takes her hours to park her car!
She's always late. Excuse me, there's my phone…

Yep, sure, I thought as much, I've got a text from old A.R. –
She'll be here… half past eight.
Well, no surprises there!
But, quite honestly, I swear,
If she wasn't my best mate,
I'd strangle her! Aw well, what's half an hour?

I'm sure the folk here look at me and think, 'That girl is sad –
Should get herself a man,'
Ach, M.A. – just sit there,
But position well your chair
So you can spot *Stefan*
And hope he'll see you too. Oh, aren't I bad?

Aw, Stefan's just a guy I see here every Friday night;
I don't mean that we meet!
No, I see him at the bar
As he's knocking back a jar
And dream it might be sweet
To raise a glass with him in this firelight!

Yes, here he comes, dead on the dot of eight, straight in the door,
His drink's a pint of stout;
I'd wander over there,
But I might lose my chair.
I pray he's here without
That awful woman he was with before!

Vous savez quoi? If he's alone, tonight I'll take a chance!
Midst all my trepidation,
A plan I have contrived –
Once Alice has arrived,
Je commencerai une conversation
Au bar avec lui, avec la confiance!

Aw, scrap *that* plan! Here comes the cow - she doesn't miss a trick!

What *does* he see in her?

He greets her every week

With a kiss upon the cheek;

She's just so...not demure!

I'm surprised his lips aren't *stuck*, her slap's so thick!

Oh, shut up, Mary Ann, I know you're starting on a rant –

But honestly, the cut of her!

I don't mean to be snooty,

But she's hardly dressed by Gucci;

And I think most would concur

She gets her clothes from Warren – *Warren Want!*

And that's not all – her laugh is like a porker on the farm!

She's loud and cheap and brassy.

He'd be better off with me -

The classy Ms Magee,

An intelligent young lassie...

Well, younger than the bit that's on his arm!

But, M.A., do snap out of this – compared to her, you're chic,
Just sip your Cabernet;
If he doesn't notice you,
Then there's nothing you can do,
Except just hope and pray
That everything will change. *Perhaps next week!*

Well, here we are again and I'm *still* sitting on my own,
Back in the Emerald Bar;
My week just seemed to drag.
Where's that phone? It's in my bag;
A.R's got trouble with her car.
Guess I'm stuck here now for ages, all alone.

It's déjà vu, right on the stroke of eight, yep – there's my man.
Hey! looking hot tonight!
But it won't be long before
She barges through that door!
Oh, she'll be here alright,
So chill out, Mary Ann, as best you can!

She's running late. Oh no, love – having problems looking *glam?*
Should have started *yesterday!*
She's a candidate, I swear,
For the next 'What Not To Wear'!
Like, Stefan, I mean to say,
If you want a change from mutton dressed as lamb...

There's *glamorous* old me (Well, skip the *old*, I'm forty-three).
I'll head toward the bar –
It's the only chance I've got,
If I lose my seat or not!
Yep, M.A. – you're a star,
So shine – it's your big opportunity!

Whoa, girl, don't move, he sees me! Is this real or am I dreaming?
Yes, he's walking over here!
'May I sit with you?' he's asking,
Oh, say, 'YES,' girl, stop that gasping!
'I've brought some wine and beer,'
Oh no – I'm sure my face is really beaming!

Right, calm down, Mary Ann – that looks like Cabernet he's bringing,

See? He's noticed what I drink;

He's ditched 'Ms I Shop Charity'

For 'la dame sophistiquee';

He's just had time to think.

Eeh! What's that awful noise? Whose phone is ringing?

Where *am* I? Where has *Stefan* gone? My thinking is oblique.

Aw...it's morning – six a.m!

That noise was such a shock,

No mobile, but my clock!

As a dream goes, what a gem,

But will it now come true? *Perhaps next week!*

*You've heard of **Team GB**. Now meet -*

Team CullyBackey!

a tale of Olympic proportions...

Current affairs and events can provide a source of inspiration for poetry, including humorous verse. I wrote this ballad just after the London 2012 Olympics and kept it on my website for quite a long time.

Those lads from Cullybackey, Jim Hughes and Billy Crowe,
(I've talked a bit about them in the past),
Were up to their old tricks, again
At the 2012 Olympics, when
They both flew into London, from Belfast.

How did they get the cash for this? I don't know – you tell me,
They must have scrimped and saved to book a flight,
But I hardly need to mention
That the boys had no intention
Of spending much – when they're not broke, they're tight!

So, they dandered up to Stratford, thinking they'd just have to pay
A fiver for a ticket through the door;
'Then we'll find a place to sleep,'
Said Jim, 'That's not too steep,
Now, let's relax. Hey, who could ask for more?'

Now, I realise we're speaking of those Cullybackey boys,
But there's something you'd think even *they* would know,
Yet it entered neither cranium
As they sauntered to the stadium
That the tickets might have sold out long ago!

So, they went and bought a programme and both took a look inside:
'See, Jim,' said Billy, 'Volleyball and Tennis
And, hey, I wouldna' mind
If the two of us could find
A seat where we can watch yon wee Jess Ennis!'

Well, they neither stopped nor stayed until they landed at the gate,
Where on duty was a steward – her badge said 'Katy';
Asked Jim, 'Have you two seats
For about a fiver each,
Or, if not, give us ones round two-pounds-eighty.'

Katy smiled and said, 'Most tickets sold out weeks ago,
Except a few, but for those, you *will* pay,
As the ones still on the rounds
Fetch a lot more than five pounds,
So I don't think that you'll get in here today.'

'We've come from Cullybackey, love, and now you're tellin' us,'
Snapped Billy, 'that our money doesn't count?'
'The tickets here are done,'
Katy said. 'Try Wimbledon –
There's a chance you might still get on Murray Mount.'

ell, the boys just stood and argued over who was meant to check
On seats and their availability
But, as neither of them knew
What the best thing was to do,
Jim said, 'Come on, let's grab a cup of tea.'

So, they headed to a cafe and sat down to work things out,
But the words exchanged between then totalled nil;
It was clear that each was huffin'
As he sat and munched his muffin,
Then, still sullen, they both shuffled to the till.

But, just as Billy turned around and headed for the door,
He said to Jim, 'Hey, do you see who's here?'
For, at a window seat
And surprisingly, quite neat,
Sat their hapless mate from Buckna, Dave McTeer.

'Whoa, Billy, don't go near yon gulpin,' Jim said. 'Let's get out,'
And tried to shove him fast towards the door;
Then they heard, above the crowd,
A familiar voice so loud,
'Hey, Jim and Billy!' from across the floor.

Of course they had no option but to turn and go back in,
And reluctantly sit down beside our Dave;
'I've a job here now,' he said,
'Working for my Uncle Ed,
So Dave the eejit's gone – I must behave!

It's magic being here in London,' Dave said. 'How's the form?
Are you here to see the Irish athletes win?'
It was over then to Billy,
Who said, 'We've both been silly
And arrived without the tickets to get in!'

'Well, boys, I think I've got a plan that might just work for you,'
Said Dave, 'but it'll take time to prepare;
If they think you're both athletes
Who have come here to compete,
They'll let you through, no problem – you'll be there!'

But, lads,' said Dave, 'for me to sort this out for you today
Will cost you both a little bit o' money –
I'll need fifty pounds from you,
Jim, the same from Billy, too –
But trust me – I'm not up to nothin' funny.'

With a lot of stifled grumbling our two lads produced the cash;

'That's our B & B tonight gone,' Billy sighed.

'Ach, never mind,' Jim said,

We can forfeit one night's bed

To get to the Olympics – right inside!'

'I'll go and get you all the gear you'll need to look the part,'

Said Dave, 'and some equipment you must bring;

Now, what sport should you play?'

Jim said, '*Fencing's* on today,

So see if you can get us anything.'

'Don't worry, lads, I'll sort you out,' said Dave, while at the till,

Then turned around and headed for the door;

'So, now I've got your cash,

As they say here, "I must dash,"

And I'll see the pair o' you back here at four.'

Well, sure enough, at four o'clock, Dave showed up on the dot,

With two huge sports bags, one on either side!

'Right, boys, go into the loo –

There's a track suit each for you,

Which you can wear with lots of Irish pride!'

Five minutes later, out they came, both looking rather cross,
In badly-fitting track suits of bright green.
'Hey, fellows, don't be mad,
It's the nearest thing they had
To the Irish gear,' said Dave. 'The choice was lean!

Now, okay – just remember, lads, to tell them who you are,
And that you're on the Irish Fencing Team.'
Well, Billy shook his head,
While Jim went kind of red
And said, 'We must be thick as clotted cream!'

'Ach, quit complainin', lads,' said Dave, 'just come and get the bags,
Then off you go, with all your sporting gear.'
'Aw, Billy, they're a ton,'
Muttered Jim, 'Try liftin' one,
And yon venue is a fair wee walk from here!'

So, they struggled to the ExCel Centre, dressed in emerald hue,
And heavy sports bags, panting all the way;
Well, hey, the looks they got,
From athletes, fans – the lot,
When finally the lads rolled up that day!

Most athletes were arriving now; the ones in front were French:
'Cabal and Marceau, 'ere for Table Tennis.'
Dressed in their smart sports jackets
And equipped with balls and racquets,
The steward just smiled, 'Good luck, Maurice and Denis.'

Now, Jim and Billy drew a breath, for they were next in line,
About the time the games were just commencing;
They defied all definition
As they queued up for admission –
'It's Hughes and Crowe, from Ireland – for the Fencing!'

'Mmm, just one moment,' said the steward, 'I'll need to check you in,
For I've not seen you at these games before.'
Then he looked them up and down
And, with one bewildered frown,
Called his boss to come and join them at the door.

Well, the manager informed them of the need to check I.D.
'Your uniform's quite... different!' he quipped.
'And no matter what your flag,
We've to check each person's bag,'
And, with that, he had their sports bags both unzipped.

'You're here to do some *Fencing,* boys? Is that why I've just found

Two *mallets* in your bags? No, I'm not wrong,

Plus *five hundred nails* at most,

With *two dozen wooden posts,*

And a *roll of barbed wire*, thirty metres long!'

Glossary:

A fair wee walk: a reasonable distance.

B&Q: a well-known chain of hardware stores.

Bann: a river flowing through Lough Neagh in the province of Ulster.

Bill Shankly: a Scottish footballer and manager, best remembered for his long tenure at Liverpool FC.

Boot (of car): 'hood' in the US.

Boots: a well-known chain of chemist shops in Ireland and the UK.

Buck eejits: silly people; similar to 'dipsticks' in the U.S.

Buckna: a small village not far from Ballymena.

Cloughmills: a village near Ballymena.

Cullybackey: a village in County Antrim, near the town of Ballymena.

Dandered: ambled, wandered.

Dead pan: expressionless.

ExCel Centre: the venue in London for the Fencing.

Galoot: *silly person; similar to 'eejit'.*

Hames: *a mess.*

'How ya dooin?': *a local greeting – 'How are you?'*

'Je commencerai une conversation, Au bar avec lui, avec la confiance!': *'I will start a conversation at the bar with him, with confidence!'*

Jess Ennis: *a well-known British track athlete.*

Kerry: *a county in South-West Ireland, at the opposite end of the island from Cullybackey.*

Maghaberry: *a prison.*

Murray Mount: *an incline just outside Wimbledon Tennis Club, where spectators can watch matches on a big screen. It is informally named after British tennis champion Andy Murray. (Alternatively called 'Henman Hill' after British tennis player Tim Henman).*

Potcheen *(Irish 'poitín'): for many years an illegal alcoholic drink, similar to 'moonshine' in the U.S.*

Quid: *slang for a pound. (Sterling, used in UK and Northern Ireland).*

Seven, eight and fifteen pound notes *(in 'The Cullybackey Counterfeiters'): these notes don't exist!*

'Speak weeth mahbles een may mowth': *talk posh, as though one had marbles in one's mouth: 'Speak with marbles in my mouth!'*

Stratford: *the location of the Olympic stadium.*

Strunt: *a huff.*

Tight: *miserly; mean; reluctant to part with money.*

'Vous savez quoi?': *'You know what?'*

Warren Want: *a play on words – 'War on Want' is the name of a chain of charity shops.*

Wee doll: *a rather dismissive term for 'young lady' in and around Belfast.*

'What Not To Wear': *a 'makeover' reality TV show in the UK.*

Wheen: *a lot.*

Yarns: *tales (usually of an exaggerated or unbelievable nature).*

Yon / thon: *that.*

Made in the USA
Charleston, SC
09 September 2016